In remembrance of

_____

*May the thoughts in this book speak to your heart
and renew your spirit in time of sorrow.*

_____

Beyond Sorrow

Christian Reflections on Death and Grief

Herb Montgomery Mary Montgomery

Blessed are those who mourn,
for they shall be comforted.
Matthew 5:4 RSV

MONTGOMERY PRESS

ACKNOWLEDGEMENTS & PERMISSIONS

Acknowledgement is made to the following for permission to reprint copyrighted material:

•Abingdon Press: REMEMBER NOW by Walter D. Cavert. Copyright renewal 1971 by Walter Cavert. Used by permission.
•Excerpt from THE JERUSALEM BIBLE, copyright © 1966 by Darton, Longman & Todd, Ltd. and Doubleday, a division of Bantam, Doubleday, Dell Publishing Group, Inc. Reprinted by permission.
•Alfred A. Knopf, Inc.: THE PROPHET by Kahlil Gibran. Copyright 1923 by Kahlil Gibran. Renewal copyright 1951 by Administrators C.T.A. of Kahlil Gibran Estate, and Mary G. Gibran. Published by Alfred A. Knopf, Inc. Reprinted with permission.
•Scripture quotations are from the REVISED STANDARD VERSION BIBLE copyright 1946, 1952, © 1971, 1973 by the Division of Christian Education of the National Council of the Churches of Christ in the USA and used by permission.
•Scripture quotations are from the NEW REVISED STANDARD VERSION BIBLE, copyright 1989 by the Division of Christian Education of the National Council of the Churches of Christ in the USA and used by permission.
•Macmillan Publishing Company: DEATH AND DYING by Elisabeth Kübler-Ross. Copyright © 1969 by Elisabeth Kübler-Ross. Reprinted with permission of Macmillan Publishing Company.
•Prentice-Hall, Inc.: NOT DEATH AT ALL by Norman Vincent Peale. © 1948, 1949, 1977. Reprinted by permission of the publisher, Prentice-Hall., Inglewood Cliffs, New Jersey.
•Fleming H. Revell Company: TURBULENT WORLD, TRANQUIL GOD by Reuben K. Youngdahl. Copyright © 1958 by Fleming H. Revell Company. Used by permission.
•Verses marked (TLB) are taken from THE LIVING BIBLE © 1971. Used by permission of Tyndale House Publishers, Inc., Wheaton, IL 60189. All rights reserved.
•Zondervan Publishing House: NO PAT ANSWERS by Eugenia Price. Copyright © 1972 by Eugenia Price. Used by permission.
•Scripture passages from: **The Jerusalem Bible** (JB), **King James Version** (KJV), **The Living Bible** (TLB), **Revised Standard Version** (RSV), **New Revised Standard Version** (NRSV).

•Photographs by Herb & Mary Montgomery

Original Edition: first printing 1977, second printing 1978, third printing 1979.
First Revised Edition: first printing 1982, second printing 1985, third printing 1987.
Second Revised Edition: first printing 1991

Copyright © 1977, 1985, 1991 by Herb & Mary Montgomery
ISBN 1-879779-01-3
Printed in the United States of America.

Montgomery Press • **P.O. Box 24124** • **Minneapolis, MN 55424**

CONTENTS

THE BEGINNING

Much as others may want to, they cannot take away your pain. They can only reassure you that there is "a right time for everything" (Ecclesiastes 3:1 TLB). This is your time to mourn in your own way. Even though it is difficult to believe this now, sorrow is not forever. There will again be a time for you to smile and be at peace, a time to take up life once more.

The Son of God said, "I have come so that they may have life and have it to the full" (John 10:10 JB). Belief in Jesus' promise does not prevent pain, despair or loneliness, but it does help us regain balance in time of sorrow. Still, our emotions—like turbulent storms—knock us off balance from time to time and swirl us from mood to deeper mood in a period of remembering and mourning.

This book contains reassuring words about the questions and the feelings that strike in both expected and unexpected moments. Familiar sights and sounds and smells can jar our memories about the person who died and leave us feeling angry and confused as well as sad. It has been this way since people first discovered love and thus felt pain when separated by death.

We sincerely hope that the thoughts we have gathered will help sustain you in your time of grief. Allow them to be touchstones for renewal of your mind and spirit. We pray that this renewal comes kindly to you as you move beyond sorrow.

The Montgomerys

WHY DID IT HAVE TO HAPPEN?

In our sorrow we seek some reason—any reason—for the death of one we loved. Often in the depths of ourselves the seeds of anger and bitterness grow until we cry out, "Why did it have to happen?" "Why did you do this to me, God?"

We might also feel great anger and bitterness toward the person who died. Perhaps the death has left us burdened with unfinished business and unrealized goals. With family responsibilities and financial problems. Anxiety and grief prompt us to direct our anger toward the deceased, and we may repeatedly demand, "Why did you die and leave me to face all this alone?"

We know our questions are unreasonable, but we have this unbearable hurt that leads us to think unsteadily. We become a different person, one we hardly recognize. Even though we know that in this life complete understanding can never be ours, we repeat the demand like a pouting child, "Why, God, why?"

A Welsh proverb states, "There are three things that only God knows: the beginning of things, the cause of things, and the end of things." God who knows the end of things may not reveal truly satisfying answers to our questions today or tomorrow or even in years to come. But we have been left with a promise that one day we will understand:

For now we see through a glass, darkly; but then face to face: now I know in part: but then shall I know even as also I am known (1 Corinthians 13:12 KJV).

Ours is a loving God who will not leave us floundering forever in confusion and questions born of grief. Even though our "whys" may go unanswered, with God's help we will emerge from our grief with a stronger spirit and our mind expanded with new understanding.

Time heals what reason cannot.

Seneca

WHERE IS GOD'S LOVE?

Day after day there is a feeling that we live in gray shadows as a continuing sense of loss engulfs us. Deprived of one we love, we see ourselves as victims. How cruel and unfair our loss seems. "Where is justice?" we ask. "Where is God's love?"

God's love is here, with us now. Difficult as it may be to understand, that love is with us each hurtful minute in our days and nights of mourning. It is the love of a God who knows and cares for us personally, a God who understands our confusion and anger and hurt. Even though we may not now believe that we will ever know happiness again, God will support us in our grief and show us the way through it.

Much of life is a mystery, and often we are frustrated by our lack of understanding. In this regard, the noted scientist Albert Einstein said, "The most beautiful thing we can experience is the mysterious."

What could be more mysterious than God? What could be more beautiful than God's replacing the gift of limited life with the gift of everlasting life?

For God so loved the world that he gave his only Son, that whoever believes in him should not perish but have eternal life (John 3:16 RSV).

God's love is with us always. It is with us now as surely as it will be when we cross into the eternal life where the very special people we knew and loved already abide in full knowledge of God's goodness and mercy.

If there were no clouds we should not enjoy the sun.

Ancient Proverb

HOW DO I SEEK GOD'S HELP?

Our life has fallen apart. Death has left a sense of despair and isolation, an isolation that extends to God. No comforting scripture comes to mind. We are too devastated even to pray. Our overwhelming sense of loss leaves us feeling abandoned and alone. We need God's help, but how do we seek it?

During this time when we are too troubled to speak clearly for ourselves, we have a spiritual partner who speaks for us:

Likewise the Spirit helps us in our weakness; for we do not know how to pray as we ought, but that very Spirit intercedes with sighs too deep for words. And God, who searches the heart, knows what is the mind of the Spirit. . . (Romans 8:26-27 NRSV).

Even though we may feel cut off from God, God is not cut off from us. The inspiring writer Eugenia Price reminds us that, "Nowhere does God promise us immunity from deep sorrow, but He did say, '. . . I am with you always.' *Not* that He would make us feel 'just fine' in a minute, but that He would be *with us*."

Perhaps we will not feel fine for some time. Possibly it will be awhile before we can turn to God in prayer. But with the knowledge that God is standing beside us in the midst of trouble, we can bear our sorrow and through it develop an even deeper faith.

One day we will appreciate the work of the Holy Spirit and be able to believe that God was involved in our healing grief even though we could not understand it at the time. Then prayer will come more easily and naturally.

IS THERE NO END TO CRYING?

In the first hours and days after a loved one dies, some of us may be so strong that people marvel at the way we handle the events and refer to us as a tower of strength. We may think that is the way we are supposed to react to a personal loss, especially if our family expects us to be strong or our loss comes at the end of a long illness. Tears may be falling on the inside, while on the outside we wear a grim mask of composure.

At some point, our emotions must have a release. The tower of steel we had forged eventually cracks and collapses. Then we weep without end. Tears fall and feelings rampage through us like floodwaters. Although we return to the routine of daily life, everything is different—different in a way that brings forth more tears. Is there no end to crying?

Abraham Lincoln not only suffered greatly but also reflected on that suffering. He wrote:

In this sad world of ours, sorrow comes to all, and it often comes with bitter agony. Perfect relief is not possible except with time. You cannot now believe that you will ever feel better. But this is not true. You are sure to be happy again. Knowing this, truly believing it, will make you less miserable now. I have had enough experience to make this statement.

Difficult as it may be to believe, there will indeed be an end to crying. Then, even though we may look back in sadness, the pain of our grief will have spent itself and happiness will again have a place in our lives.

When pain is to be borne,
a little courage helps more than much knowledge . . .
C.S. Lewis

WHERE DO I TURN?

One of the important people in our life is gone, and death has left us burdened with worry and confusion. Our mind spins. The days of familiar and comfortable activities have been turned upside down. We are devastated by uncertainty and yearn for an oasis of calm where we can be renewed and restored. What can we do about it? Where can we turn for help when we need the strength to prepare a meal, answer someone's questions or go about another pressing activity that must be faced?

We might find the help we need by turning to the 23rd Psalm and looking to the Shepherd who loves and cares for us everlastingly:

The Lord is my shepherd; I shall not want. He maketh me to lie down in green pastures: he leadeth me beside the still waters. He restoreth my soul: he leadeth me in the paths of righteousness for his name's sake. Yea, though I walk through the valley of the shadow of death, I will fear no evil: for thou art with me: thy rod and thy staff they comfort me. Thou preparest a table before me in the presence of mine enemies: thou anointest my head with oil; my cup runneth over. Surely goodness and mercy shall follow me all the days of my life: and I will dwell in the house of the Lord forever (KJV).

The Good Shepherd protects the old as well as the young, and seeks the return of any who feel lost or out of touch. The Shepherd never turns away from us. Always the Shepherd turns toward us with openness, inviting, "Come unto me . . . "

God does not take away trials
or carry us over them,
but rather strengthens us through them.
E.B. Pusey

WILL I ALWAYS FEEL GUILTY?

Guilt whispers through us. It grows until we feel an agony of remorse and regret. There are those things we wish we hadn't done, and unkind words we wish we hadn't spoken. Just as troublesome as what we did and said are the things we didn't do, the words we didn't say.

Too often in the past we let our loving feelings go unexpressed. We should have touched more gently and spoken with greater concern. We could have listened with our full attention and loved more completely, but the days were busy and we were preoccupied with our own lives. It was so easy to let time slip away because we believed there was always going to be another tomorrow for us.

Now that it is tomorrow—and too late—we rail at ourselves. Guilt saps us of energy. We toss about as we seek the peace of sleep. On and on questions of "Why did I . . . ?" and "Why didn't I . . . ?" come as if they will never end. But end they will. Among the insightful writings of the poet Ella Wheeler Wilcox are these assuring words that we will eventually find peace with ourselves:

> **This, too, will pass away: absorb the thought,**
> **And wait—your waiting will not be in vain,**
> **The dark today leads into light tomorrow:**
> **There is no endless joy, no endless sorrow.**

As time diminishes our grief, the hurtful past will fade. Our inner whisperings about "What should have been" or "What might have been" will grow ever fainter. In their place will be fond memories to cherish.

WHAT ABOUT CONDEMNATION?

We may be anxious about the destiny of one who has died, especially if the person for whom we grieve did not appear to be very religious in the eyes of the world. Our distress runs deep as we think of heaven and hell, saint and sinner, good and bad.

Compassion should be ours, for who among us is all good or all bad? When some men were about to put to death a woman they called a sinner, it was a merciful Jesus who said, "Let him who is without sin among you be the first to throw a stone at her" (John 8:7 RSV). No stones were thrown that day.

In another instance Jesus admonished, "Judge not, that you be not judged" (Matthew 7:1 RSV).

There may, however, be people who pass harsh judgment on the one we mourn. As much as possible, we must ignore what is said. Those whose comments create pain are to be pitied for their lack of charity. Undoubtedly they live without an image of a compassionate God.

Surely much is hidden from us now. What lies after death is largely unknown, but we gain insight and hope as we ponder these reassuring words of Jesus:

Do not let your hearts be troubled. Trust in God still, and trust in me. There are many rooms in my Father's house; if there were not, I should have told you. I am going now to prepare a place for you, and after I have gone and prepared you a place, I shall return to take you with me; so that where I am you may be too (John 14:1-3 JB).

God, who is all loving and all merciful, has a place prepared for each of us. Therein lies our peace of mind and heart.

*H*is mercy endureth forever.

Chronicles 16:34 KJV

WHAT COMES AFTER DEATH?

Some of us worry about what may or may not lie beyond death. The word of God is clear, but still we wonder, "What if there is nothing?"

Let us not forget the natural order of this changing world. Rivers become oceans. Seeds become plants. Caterpillars become butterflies. If we will but open our senses, there is order to be observed, purpose to be discovered and transformation to be experienced.

Professor, pastor and writer Walter Dudley Cavert expressed his thoughts about transformation with helpful insight:

In the bottom of an old pond lived some grubs who could not understand why none of their group ever came back after crawling up the stems of the lilies to the top of the water. They promised each other that the next one who was called to make the upward climb would return and tell what happened to him. Soon one of them felt an urgent impulse to seek the surface; he rested himself on the top of a lily pad and went through a glorious transformation which made him a dragonfly with beautiful wings. In vain he tried to keep his promise. Flying back and forth over the pond, he peered down at his friends below. Then he realized that even if they could see him they would not recognize such a radiant creature as one of their number.

The fact that we cannot see our friends or communicate with them after the transformation, which we call death, is no proof that they cease to exist.

Ours is a creative God, the maker of heaven and earth and all that lives on it. This God who is the giver of life most assuredly has a creative destiny for us beyond death.

The Lord is near to the broken-hearted, and saves the crushed in spirit.
Psalms 34:18 RSV

IS DEATH AN ENDING OR A BEGINNING?

Although we long to believe God's promise that death is a passage to a new life, our thoughts of what lies beyond this life are tinged with fear of the unknown. Today, however, we have the benefit of information that makes the unknown less fearful than it once seemed to be. In recent times, many apparently dead persons have come back to life. Emergency medical procedures brought some back. Others who were pronounced dead simply returned to life.

When Dr. Carl Jung appeared to have died of a heart attack, he experienced what he later called one of the most meaningful events of his life. Like many others who have had similar experiences, Jung felt released from his physical body. He was pulled back into it only when emergency measures were taken by his doctor.

In another instance, an American woman believes that she had to die in order to learn how to live. Now, in her new life, this young wife and mother says that "every morning is like Easter." A Canadian man who was declared clinically dead had a glimpse of eternity. Upon being revived, he told his doctors that what he had experienced was so beautiful that he did not want them to try to revive him if it happened again.

In case after case, those who return to this life report having seen beautiful light; light more pure, more bright, more colorful than anything known before. They come back serene and free of the fear of death. These people also tell of peace, joy and a comforting presence. They speak of having "seen behind the closed door." Such experiences reassure us that death is not a fearful ending. Instead, it appears to be a wonderful new beginning—a passage from one life to another just as Christ promised.

God of life, there are days
when the burdens we carry
chafe our shoulders and wear us down;
when the road seems dreary and endless,
the skies grey and threatening;
when our lives have no music in them,
and our hearts are lonely,
and our souls have lost their courage.
Flood the path with light, we beseech Thee;
turn our eyes to where the skies are full of promise....
Augustine

WILL I EVER ACCEPT?

We cannot quite believe that death has occurred. For a time we may block out the event and pretend the death never happened. We think of it as a bad dream from which we will awaken to find life as it was.

Our daydreams and fanciful imaginings keep away the reality of permanent separation. The ring of the phone startles us, and we wonder if the person for whom we grieve might be on the line. The mail carrier comes. Could there be a letter? Some sunny morning won't the person we miss so greatly come walking down the street and appear at the door?

We all have our own time and way of accepting the death of someone whose life has been an important part of ours. For some of us, acceptance comes rather soon. For others, it takes much longer. Years even. But eventually acceptance does come to each of us. This understanding was poignantly captured by a ten-year-old girl in her poem:

MY GRANDFATHER
When I was young
after my grandfather died
I saw his hat and told my mom
that he had forgotten it.
He had to come back and get it.
Now I know
he never will.

When we are able to say, "thy will be done," we accept life as it is, not as we would like it to be. Peace of heart and mind will soon follow.

Oh, write of me, not "Died in bitter pains,"

But "Emigrated to another star!"
Helen Hunt Jackson

DOES GOD HEAR MY PRAYERS?

Time passes and we have tried to pray, but it has not seemed to help. We feel that praying is useless, that God is not listening any more.

Does God hear our prayers? It is a question we have all asked from time to time. For the answer, we look to the words of Jesus when he promised, "Ask, and it will be given to you; seek, and you will find; knock, and it will be opened to you. For everyone who asks receives . . . " (Matthew 7:7-8 RSV).

Norman Vincent Peale tells about the prayers of a man who had been outgoing and highly successful in business. At home this man depended heavily on his wife. For years she had led their prayers each evening when they knelt and joined hands. After his wife died, the husband felt like a scared and lost child. Finally he prayed:

"O God . . . You know how much I need you. I put my life in your hands. Help me, dear Lord."

Then the man related how he felt a touch on his hand, the hand his wife had always held when they prayed. **"It was a strong, kindly touch," he said, "and I seemed to feel a great hand take my own. In surprise, I looked up, but, of course, could see no one. However all the pain seemed to go out of my mind and peace came into my heart. I knew that God was with me and would never leave me. . . . "**

God responds to all who pray and open themselves to loving answers. Will our answer be so dramatic that we feel touched? Or will our response come in another way? We won't know until we place ourselves completely in God's protective care.

IS IT WORTH PICKING UP THE PIECES?

The separation caused by death leaves us with a sense of futility and hopelessness. We feel splintered, broken into shards which appear to have no chance of ever being refitted into anything useful or beautiful.

Someone we love has passed on and we feel crushed by the emptiness death leaves. Thoughts of self-destruction may enter our mind. The idea of ending our own life shames us but attracts us too. Wouldn't we be better off dead? The question leads us to a sense of isolation. We try to recall others who have rebuilt their lives on the shambles of despair. Is it worth picking up the pieces of our lives again? Reuben K. Youngdahl, the noted minister and writer, believed that it is. After the destruction Europe suffered in WWII, he wrote:

During the war, the rose window in the great Rheims cathedral was shattered into bits by an indirect hit. The parishoners lovingly got down on their hands and knees to gather together all the tiny pieces of broken glass. When the war was over, they hired the most skilled workmen available to rebuild it, piece by piece, from the gathered fragments. Today's rose window in Rheims is more beautiful than it ever was. So God can take our broken lives and reshape them.

Though death has shattered our lives, we can pick up the pieces. Having picked them up and put them back together, we can resume life as someone to whom sorrow has given new wisdom and beauty of spirit.

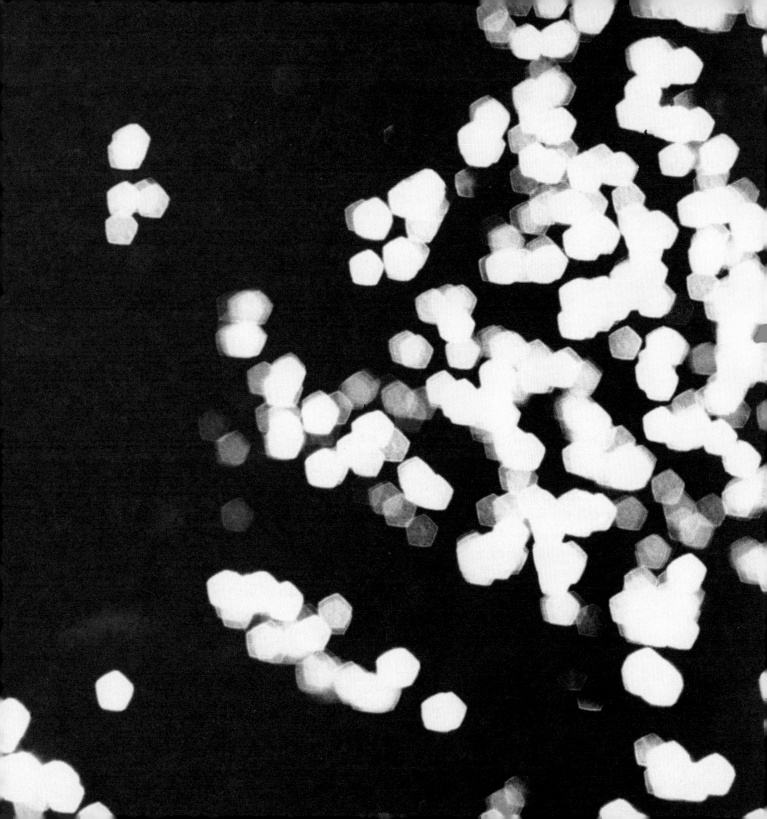

*The deeper that sorrow
carves into your being,
the more joy you can contain.*
Kahlil Gibran

HOW LONG WILL I DRIFT?

Alone, we question our values and direction. We see no goal. It is frightening to grope in darkness. How long will we drift? The way had seemed clear, but now as we reflect, we wonder about the goals we had before this death. We ask ourselves, "Was I only a follower?" "Did someone else set my course?" "What values do I have?" "What is my new direction to be?"

If listlessness overcomes us, self-pity tags along. It consumes our thoughts, and life seems futile. We avoid action and plunge into gloom that prevents us from seeing new possibilities. This is a time to be patient, for time will redirect our steps.

When we reflect upon what has happened to us, we realize that—despite the pain of grief—we are still capable of growing, giving, loving. Even in our time of sorrow is there not some other person for whom we might provide comfort and stability? Perhaps there is a child or adult, a relative or friend, who needs our reassurance. There is surely someone whose struggles could be less painful if we would choose to give of ourselves. In giving we can reestablish a direction and realize the wisdom in the words of Confucius:

It is better to light one small candle than to curse the darkness.

Although an act of caring on our part is a small thing, it is a beginning. Through that beginning we may discover renewed meaning. We will not necessarily find our new direction immediately, but making a conscious decision to reach out to others gets us moving again with determination and purpose.

Our main business
is not to see what lies dimly at a distance,
but to do what lies clearly at hand.
Thomas Carlyle

WHERE ARE MY FRIENDS?

After a while no one seems to weep with us anymore. Cards, letters and sympathy calls come infrequently. Have friends already forgotten our loss? Have they rejected us in our misery?

Although the mourning of our friends has ended sooner than ours, they have not forgotten us. They are waiting, waiting for us to return our attention to the mainstream of life and to the activities we have neglected.

Withdrawal, which often accompanies grief, creates a great need to share. But sharing is not always easy. We may be embarrassed or ashamed to admit our loneliness, our guilt, our sense of despair. And so it is that we hold back, refraining from making contact with those we call friends.

Ralph Waldo Emerson penned a definition that is worth pondering:

A friend is a person with whom I may be sincere.

As we think about people who have been our friends, we can choose one who matches Emerson's definition. Hesitant as we may be to take the initiative, we can find encouragement in the scripture that urges us to "be not frightened, neither be dismayed; for ... your God is with you" (Joshua 1:9 RSV).

Contacting a friend will, for the moment, take the focus off ourselves and thereby lessen our grief. In time we will be less concerned with what friends can do for us and more concerned with what we can do to put warmth and mutual support into our relationships. Becoming less self-centered enables us to once again be a true friend to those who need us.

When sorrow overwhelms me
and no one seems able to help,
I retreat to nature.
There I rediscover God's healing
in the whisper of the wind.
Though I still hurt, I know I will survive,
for when I am in touch with the earth,
I am in touch with myself and my God.

Kimo

WILL SOME GOOD COME OF IT?

There are those who tell us some good will come of the grief we are experiencing. Others may say that what has happened is all for the best and that our loss is serving a worthy and useful purpose. Our thoughts rebel at such ideas! What good could come of the death of one we loved? What good could come of our pain and loneliness?

If we find answers to these questions at all, they will come slowly. For now it is important to remember that neither darkness nor the storm last forever. And when light and calm have reentered our lives, it is time to consider how sorrow has affected us. Perhaps we will discover that we are stronger than we once thought. Death may very well increase our sensitivity and lead us to another, richer level of belief.

What we take from the experience will be as personal as our grief. In some small measure it is a comfort just to know that we have lived through it. We have made it this far. Possibly, as we move beyond sorrow, we will have new insights into death and its relationship to life. The research and writings of Dr. Elisabeth Kübler-Ross have encouraged people to share their thoughts and feelings about death:

It might be helpful if more people would talk about death and dying as an intrinsic part of life just as they do not hesitate to mention when someone is expecting a new baby.

Although it is as natural to die as it is to be born, death is a departure from life as we know it. It is a painful separation. Our grief is a sign that we have loved, and eventually good always comes of love.

In short there are three things that last:
faith, hope and love;
and the greatest of these is love.
1 Corinthians 13:13 JB

WHAT WILL TOMORROW BRING?

As time passes, we continue to be disorganized and put off tasks that need doing. An uneasy feeling lingers. Alone and unoccupied, we still fret about yesterday. We know we cannot undo the past, yet we become victims of regretful thoughts. "If only we had known of the sickness earlier." "If only she hadn't driven that day." "If only we'd had one last talk."

Yesterday is gone. Tomorrow does not yet belong to us. All we really have is today, and with our todays we can fashion a future for ourselves. For a time, death may obscure the purpose of our life, but it does not diminish us as unique persons created in God's image.

Instead of asking anxiously, "What will tomorrow bring?" we might better ask, "What will I bring to tomorrow?" Young or old, each of us has something special to give. Some talent, some skill, some understanding, some loving quality. What we do with our abilities will enhance today and affect tomorrow. The poet Henry Wadsworth Longfellow suggested a wise and comforting course when he wrote:

Look not mournfully into the Past. It comes not back again. Wisely improve the Present. It is thine. Go forth to meet the shadowy Future, without fear . . .

We must be ever mindful that we do not live our todays or face our tomorrows alone. God is always with us. And, "with God all things are possible" (Mark 10:27 KJV). If we ask God's help in giving the best that we have to today, we can meet our tomorrows with courage and the hope of renewed happiness.

What we have once enjoyed
we can never lose.
All that we love deeply
becomes a part of us.
Helen Keller